1 Introduction

A number of studies purport to show that particular human resource practices are complementary and lead to higher firm performance, for example Appelbaum et al. (2000) and Ichniowski et al. (1997). These "high performance work systems" include employee involvement programs like self-managed work teams, incentive programs like profit sharing and other human resource practices like formal training programs. This paper analyzes the firm's choice of two important human resource practices: self-managed work teams and formal training programs. The paper shows that the value of individual practices to a firm depends on characteristics of the firm's product market, and on the choice of other practices by the firm. In particular, conditional on the use of training programs, firms that produce custom products value the use of teams more highly than firms that don't produce custom products, and firms value the use of teams and the use of training in a way that is consistent with the two practices being complements.

The paper analyzes a theoretical model and illustrates the mechanism via which the use of two human resource practices (self-managed work teams and formal training programs) increase firm productivity. Analysis of the model gives two main results. First, it shows that self-managed work teams increase productivity of firms with substantial volatility in the types of orders produced, by allowing faster decision making. Second, it shows that for workers in teams, formal training programs increase the accuracy of their information, allowing them to make better choices. These two results form the basis for the paper's two hypotheses. First, firms value teams more when orders are customized to individual customer needs. Second, teams and training programs are complements. The empirical model allows the firm to choose both self-managed work teams and formal training programs simultaneously. The model also allows for the possibility that the two practices are complements, while not requiring that the firm choose "systems" of practices. The empirical results are consistent with the theoretical model, giving further insight into the firm's motivation for selecting high performance work systems.

The paper contributes to the theoretical literature on the use of self-managed work teams and formal training programs. It does so by presenting a model of the firm's decision making process and analyzing the impact of teams and training on the effectiveness of the process. Previous work analyzed the value of self-managed work teams when they are combined with profit sharing (Adams (2001); Che and Yoo (Forthcoming); Drago (1995); Kandel and Lazear (1992)). However, there is no work on the direct value of teams. The analysis presented below is related to the "team theoretic" literature on decision making in firms. The focus of that work is on the optimal size and structure of the firm given time and communication constraints.[1] The focus of the analysis below is on choosing the *optimal decision maker* given informational differences between decision makers and assuming communication constraints between decision makers.

The decision making environment is characterized as a dynamic decision making problem under uncertainty. Rustichini and Wolinsky (1995) present a relatively simple model of such a problem. This paper uses a slightly more general version in which the decision maker observes noisy signals of outcomes. Their model and results serve as the limiting case. The model is a countable state Markov decision making problem, important results for which are described in Puterman (1994).[2]

The paper contributes to the empirical literature on the use of work practices in two ways (Black and Lynch (1998); Jones and Pliskin (1997); Osterman (1994, 1995); Whitfield (2000)). First, by using an empirical model that allows the two practices (self-managed work teams and formal training programs) to be chosen simultaneously. Second by using an empirical model that allows the two choices to interact (and for this interaction to vary with observable characteristics of the firm). The approach used in this paper, generalizes the approach adopted by Jones and Pliskin (1997) who analyze the use of human resource practices in Canadian manufacturing firms. Jones

---

[1] See Borland and Eichberger (1998) for an overview of the team theoretic literature.

[2] Results for finite state Markov decision making problems are described in Derman (1970). Results for more general dynamic decision making problems are described in Stokey and Lucas (1989).

and Pliskin (1997) allow the firm to choose two individual practices simultaneously. The approach used in this paper allows a richer structure in which practices are chosen simultaneously and observable characteristics can affect the interaction between choices of practices. This more general model allows the paper to explicitly test the hypothesis that self-managed work teams and formal training programs are complements.

The rest of the paper proceeds as follows. Section 2 presents a theoretical analysis of the firm's decision to use high performance work systems. A model of dynamic decision making under uncertainty is used to analyze the value of using self-managed work teams and formal training programs. Section 3 presents an empirical model that allows the firm to choose multiple practices simultaneously and for those practices to be complements. The section presents two hypotheses based upon the theoretical analysis. The first hypothesis states that self-managed work teams are more valuable to the firm when there is volatility in the types of orders on the firm's production line. The second hypothesis states that self-managed work teams and formal training programs are complements. Section 4 discusses the data set which is based on a large economy wide survey of U.S. manufacturing establishments. The section also discusses the measures that are used to test the hypotheses. Section 5 discusses the empirical results, which give support for the two main hypotheses. Section 6 concludes.

2 Theoretical Model

This section presents a model that can be used to determine the value of high performance work systems. The model is based on a dynamic decision making problem under uncertainty (Rustichini and Wolinsky (1995)). The section presents two propositions. The first proposition states that conditional on the use of training programs, for firms facing volatility in the types of orders on the production line, there is greater value in giving substantive decision making power to production line workers. The second proposition states that the use of training programs increases the value of giving decision making power to production line workers. These two propositions form the basis for the hypotheses presented in the next section.

2.1 The Model

The firm chooses whether or not to use teams and whether or not to use formal training. I assume that the use of teams corresponds with choosing an "on-line" decision maker (as opposed to an "off-line" decision maker. An on-line decision maker is someone like a production line worker who is physically located on the production line. An off-line decision maker is someone like a production manager or production engineer who is physically located away from the production line (in their office for example).[3] while the use of formal training programs increases the accuracy of the information available to the on-line decision maker. The value of some combination of teams and training is denoted, V_{MR} where $M = 1$ if teaMs are used and $M = 0$ if teams are not used, and $R = 1$ if tRaining is used and $R = 0$ if training is not used. Whomever the firm gives decision making power to, their problem is as follows:

1. At period $t = 0$, the firm chooses $(M, R) \in \{(0,0), (1,0), (0,1), (1,1)\}$ to maximize

$$V_{MR} = \sum_{t=0}^{\infty} \delta_f^t E(\pi_t(\tau_t, s_t)|\omega_0 : \sigma_{MRt}, \gamma_R) \qquad (1)$$

where $\delta_f \in (0, 1)$ is the firm's discount factor, $\pi_t \in \{0, 1\}$ is the payoff in period t, $\tau_t \in \{0, 1\}$ is the task choice of the decision maker in period t, $s_t \in \{0, 1\}$ is the state of the world in period t, $\omega_t = \Pr(s_t = 1)$ is the firm's belief about the state of the world, $\sigma_{MRt} \in \{0, 1\}$ is the decision maker's signal of the state of the world, and $\gamma_R \in (0, 1)$ is a parameter capturing the amount of noise there is in the decision maker's signal.

2. At the beginning of period t the decision maker has a belief about that state of the world, such that $\omega_t' = \Pr(s_t = 1)$.

---

[3] See Drago (1995), Levine (1995) or Eaton et al. (1997) for a discussion of the different types of employee involvement.

3. The decision maker observes a signal of the state of world, σ_{MRt}, and updates her belief via Bayes' Rules, $\omega_t = \Pr(s_t = 1|\sigma_{MRt}, \omega'_t)$.

4. Given, ω_t, the decision maker chooses a task, τ_t to optimize

$$U_t = \sum_{j=t}^{\infty} \delta_d^{j-t} E(\pi_j(\tau_j, s_j)|\omega_t) \tag{2}$$

where $\delta_d \in (0,1)$ is the decision maker's discount rate.

5. The payoff at time t, is a function of the task and the state.

$$\pi_t(\tau_t, s_t) = \begin{cases} 1 \text{ with probability } k \text{ if } \tau_t = 0 \\ 0 \text{ with probability } 1-k \text{ if } \tau_t = 0 \\ 1 \text{ with probability } \omega_t \text{ if } \tau_t = 1 \\ 0 \text{ with probability } 1-\omega_t \text{ if } \tau_t = 1 \end{cases} \tag{3}$$

where $k \in (0,1)$ is some constant.

6. In the next period, $t+1$, the probability the state changes is $\alpha = \Pr(s_{t+1} = 1|s_t = 0) = \Pr(s_{t+1} = 0|s_t = 1) \in (0, .5)$.

7. The decision maker updates her belief, $\omega'_{t+1} = \Pr(s_{t+1} = 1|\omega_t)$.

If the firm chooses $M = 0$, then $\sigma_{01t} = \sigma_{00t} = s_{t-2}$. That is, if no teams are used, the decision maker observes the exact state of the world two periods ago. Adams (2001) shows that there exists an optimal "cutoff" strategy. If two assumptions are made, then the value of the firm's choice can be written as follows

$$V_{00} = V_{01} = \frac{1 + (1-2\alpha)^2 + 2k}{4} \tag{4}$$

where $\Pr(s_t = 1|s_{t-2} = 1) = \frac{1+(1-2\alpha)^2}{2}$. The first assumption is that α is small enough that the decision maker never chooses the same task (τ_t) in every period t. This assumption is made for ease of exposition. The second assumption is that δ_f is close to 1. This assumption corresponds to the idea that the firm consider's the "long run" in making its choice about the best decision maker.[4] Adams (2001) shows that if δ_f is close to 1, then it is equivalent to evaluating the decision maker by the "long run" average expected payoff. Equation (4) shows that in the long run the off-line decision maker chooses task $\tau_t = 1$ half of the time and the state is 1 with probability $\frac{1+(1-2\alpha)^2}{2}$. Note that this probability is decreasing in α. The other half of the time, the off-line decision maker chooses $\tau_t = 0$ and the expected payoff is k.

If the firm chooses $M = 1$ and $R = 0$, then $\sigma_{10t} = \gamma_0 \pi_{t-1} + (1 - \gamma_0)(1 - \pi_{t-1})$. If $M = 1$ and $R = 1$, then $\sigma_{11t} = \gamma_1 \pi_{t-1} + (1 - \gamma_1)(1 - \pi_{t-1})$, where $\gamma_1 > \gamma_0$. The decision maker observes a noisy signal of the previous period's payoff where the level of noise depends on whether or not training is also used. Adams (2001) shows that there exists an optimal "cutoff" strategy. It is assumed that α is small enough and γ_R is large enough that it is *not* optimal for the decision maker to choose the same task τ_t in every period t. Rustichini and Wolinsky (1995) analyze the case where $\gamma_1 = 1$, and show

$$V_{11} = \frac{2N\alpha k + 1 - (1 - 2\alpha)^N}{2(N+1)\alpha + 1 - (1 - 2\alpha)^N} \quad (5)$$

where N is the number of times in a row that $\tau_t = 1$. The case where $\gamma_R < 1$ is left to the appendix.

In summary, the choice of teams is modelled as a choice to use a noisy and indirect signal of the previous periods state as opposed to a noiseless and direct signal of the state two periods ago. The choice of training is modelled as a choice to increase the accuracy of the indirect signal of the state. This representation corresponds with the observation that when teams are used, production line workers are given substantive decision making power over how to run the line (Drago (1995); Levine (1995)). While these workers are right on the production line, they often lack significant levels of education or training. In the model, the on-line decision maker is learning by doing, as the informativeness of the signal she observe depends on the choices she makes. The alternative decision making structure is the more traditional one in which the choice of production method is made by highly trained production managers and production engineers. While these decision makers have

---

[4]Rustichini and Wolinsky (1995) use this idea.

accurate information, that information may be subject to significant delay as these decision makers are not on the production line. Training programs increase the worker's ability to make good choices given the information she observes.

2.2 Results

There are two main theoretical results. The first result states that conditional upon whether training programs are used, teams are more valuable to the firm when the probability that the state will change from period to period is high (α is high), relative to the case when the probability that the state will change from period to period is low (α is low). The second result states that training increases the value of using teams. These two results are presented as Proposition 1 and Proposition 2, respectively.

Proposition 1   *1. There exists α_L, α_H such that $\alpha_L < \alpha_H$ and if $\alpha_l < \alpha_L$ and $\alpha_H < \alpha_h$ then*

$$V_{10}(\alpha_l) - V_{00}(\alpha_l) < V_{10}(\alpha_h) - V_{00}(\alpha_h) \tag{6}$$

2. There exists α'_L, α'_H such that $\alpha'_L < \alpha'_H$ and if $\alpha_l < \alpha'_L$ and $\alpha'_H < \alpha_h$ then

$$V_{11}(\alpha_l) - V_{01}(\alpha_l) < V_{11}(\alpha_h) - V_{01}(\alpha_h) \tag{7}$$

Proof. In the appendix.

Part (1) of the proposition states that conditional on *not* using training, the firm values teams relatively higher when α is relatively large. Part (2) of the proposition states that conditional on using training, the firm values teams relatively higher when α is relatively large. The proof of this proposition is based upon a result of Rustichini and Wolinsky (1995) which states that α converges to 0, there is incomplete learning by the decision maker whose information is based upon their action choices (the one with teams in this case). It is shown that for the alternative case (where there is no teams and information is not conditional on action choices), there is *no* incomplete learning as α approaches 0. At the other end, when α is large, the delay associated with the off-line decision maker makes her information poor relative to the on-line decision maker.

Intuitively, when α is small there is little variation in the state and the off-line decision maker's information remains good. However, the on-line decision maker is learning by doing, the implication of which is that she may get "trapped" making the wrong choice. This occurs because the outcome from that choice is not informing her of the true state, and she does not switch to the correct choice. On the other hand, when α is large the off-line decision maker's information deteriorates very quickly, and the on-line decision maker has more accurate information.

Proposition 2 $V_{00} + V_{11} > V_{10} + V_{01}$

Proof In the appendix.

Proposition 2 states that self-managed work teams and formal training programs are "super-modular" in the firm's value function and thus are complements (Athey and Stern (1998); Milgrom and Roberts (1990)). The proof of the proposition is based on the assumption that when self-managed teams are used formal training programs increase the accuracy of the on-line decision maker's information and thus the expected value of the decision maker's choices. However, if teams are not used, then formal training programs will have no affect on the accuracy of the (off-line) decision maker's information and thus the expected value of the decision maker's choices will not change.

The next section presents the empirical model used to test the hypotheses.

3 Empirical Model

This section presents the empirical model that is used to test the implications of the theoretical model presented above. The model is a latent profit model. There are three subsections. The first subsection presents the notation for a linear latent profit model. The second subsection presents the restrictions imposed on the structure of the firm's latent profits by the theoretical model and the hypotheses to be tested in the empirical section. The third subsection presents the estimated model, including a description of distributional assumptions.

3.1 Linear Latent Profit Model

There exist four possible choices for the firm, the latent value of each is presented below. V_{MR} is the latent value to the firm, where M indicates whether teaMs are used by the firm and R indicates whether tRaining is used by the firm. First, the value of neither using teams nor training is denoted by A_i for firm i. The latent profits of the other choices will be compared to this one.

$$V_{00} = A_i \tag{8}$$

The value of using teams but not using training is V_{10}. The relative value of this choice is a function of the measure of how much volatility there is on the firm's production floor, $X_{i\alpha}$, and of other characteristics of the firm (X_i). V_{10} is also affected by unobservable characteristics of the firm (ϵ_{iM}).

$$V_{10} = A_i + X_{i\alpha}\beta_{\alpha M} + X_i\beta_{iM} + \epsilon_{iM} \tag{9}$$

The value of using training but not teams is V_{01}.

$$V_{01} = A_i + X_{i\alpha}\beta_{\alpha R} + X_i\beta_{iR} + \epsilon_{iR} \tag{10}$$

where ϵ_{iR} represents unobservable characteristics that affect the relative value of using training only. The other variables are defined above. The value of both teams and training is V_{11}.

$$V_{11} = A_i + X_{i\alpha}\beta_{\alpha MR} + X_i\beta_{iMR} + \epsilon_{iMR} \tag{11}$$

where ϵ_{iMR} represents the unobservable characteristics that affect the relative value of using both teams and training. Again the other variables are defined above.

One of the main objectives of the empirical analysis is measuring the complementarity between using teams and using training programs. If the two practices are complements then they are super-modular in the firm's latent profits (Athey and Stern (1998); Milgrom and Roberts (1990)). This implies that,

$$V_{00} + V_{11} \geq V_{01} + V_{10} \tag{12}$$

To see the implications of this assumption, and measure the factors that affect the complementarity, it is easier to rewrite Equation (11) in the following way, where the $\beta*_{MR}$ variables are substituted for equivalent $\beta_{MR} - \beta_M - \beta_R$ variables.

$$\begin{aligned}V_{11} = A_i + X_{i\alpha}\beta_{\alpha M} + X_i\beta_{iM} + \epsilon_{iM} + X_{i\alpha}\beta_{\alpha R} + X_i\beta_{iR} + \epsilon_{iR} \\ + X_{i\alpha}\beta*_{\alpha MR} + X_i\beta*_{iMR} + \epsilon*_{iMR}\end{aligned} \tag{13}$$

Therefore, $\beta*_{iMR} = \beta_{iMR} - \beta_{iM} - \beta_{iR}$ and $\epsilon*_{iMR} = \epsilon_{iMR} - \epsilon_{iM} - \epsilon_{iR}$. In this sense, the $\beta*$ coefficients determine the "extra" value of having both practices together. If $\epsilon*_{iMR} = 0$, then Equation (12) holds if and only if

$$X_{i\alpha}\beta*_{\alpha MR} + X_i\beta*_{iMR} \geq 0 \tag{14}$$

3.2 Hypotheses

Proposition 1 states that conditional on the use of training programs firms value the use of teams more highly for high values of α relative to low values of α. The appropriate differences in the empirical model are

$$V_{10} - V_{00} = X_{i\alpha}\beta_{\alpha M} + X_i\beta_{iM} + \epsilon_{iM} \tag{15}$$

and

$$V_{11} - V_{01} = X_{i\alpha}\beta_{\alpha M} + X_i\beta_{iM} + \epsilon_{iM} + X_{i\alpha}\beta*_{\alpha MR} + X_i\beta*_{iMR} + \epsilon*_{iMR} \tag{16}$$

The empirical model presented above assumes that the firm's value of teams is linear in the measure of α, therefore the proposition implies the following hypothesis.

Hypothesis 1 1. $\frac{\partial(V_{10}-V_{00})}{\partial X_\alpha} = \beta_{\alpha M} > 0$

2. $\frac{\partial(V_{11}-V_{01})}{\partial X_\alpha} = \beta_{\alpha M} + \beta*_{\alpha MR} > 0$

Part (1) of the hypothesis states that conditional on not using training, the firm values the use of teams more highly when the measure of α is higher. Part (2) of the hypothesis states that condition on the use of training, the firm values the use of teams more highly when the measure of α is higher.

Proposition 2 states that teams and training programs are complements. The appropriate inequality is Equation (14). Assuming that the measures $X_{i\alpha}$ and X_i are positive (which they are in this case), the proposition implies the following hypothesis.

Hypothesis 2 $\beta*_{\alpha MR} + \beta*_{iMR} > 0$

The hypothesis states that the "extra" effect of having both practices together is positive for every firm. The measures used to test this hypothesis are discussed below. It would be preferable to know whether the workers receiving training were the same workers that are involved in teams, unfortunately this information is not available in this data set.

3.3 Estimated Model

This subsection presents the empirical model of the firm's decision to use teams and training. The model allows the firm's choice on teams and training to be made simultaneously, and it allows the two choices to interact. The model's key characteristic is that it allows this interaction to vary from firm to firm in observable ways. In order to make the estimation of this model tractable it is assumed that the unobservables $\{\epsilon_M, \epsilon_R\}$ are distributed standard bivariate normally where the correlation is represented by ρ.[5] As a

---

[5]This includes the assumption that $\epsilon*_{iMR} = 0$ or $\epsilon_{iMR} = \epsilon_{iM} + \epsilon_{iR}$. Adams (2001) presents a model which allows a third error term ϵ_{iMR}, however it is significantly more difficult to estimate.

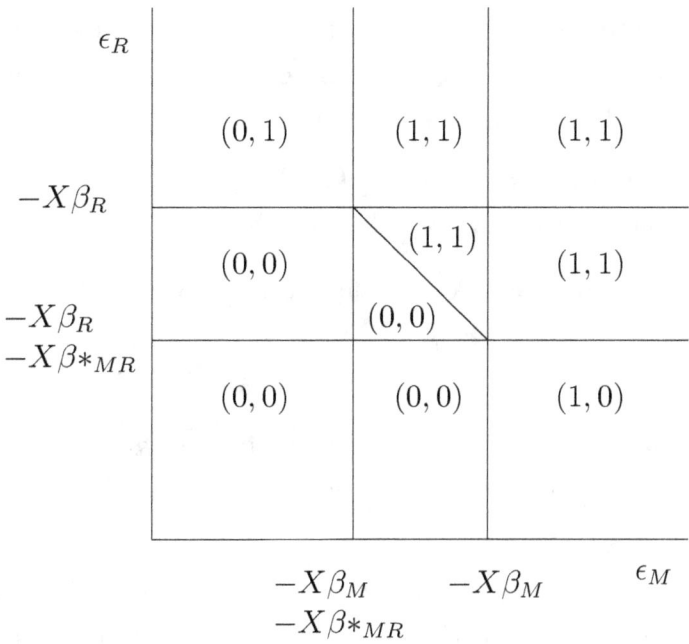

Figure 1: The State Space

consequence of this assumption, the likelihood function is not continuous unless it is either assumed that

$$X_{i\alpha}\beta*_{\alpha MR} + X_i\beta*_{iMR} \geq 0 \tag{17}$$

or it is assumed that

$$X_{i\alpha}\beta*_{\alpha MR} + X_i\beta*_{iMR} \leq 0 \tag{18}$$

Therefore, in this paper, it is further assumed that Equation (14) holds (with a weak inequality). Note that if this equation is actually 0 for all i, then the model is equivalent to the standard bivariate probit model. The implication is that the choice of one practice cannot *decrease* the latent profits from the other practice.

Figure 1 depicts the state space over ϵ_M and ϵ_R. It can be seen that as $X\beta*_{MR}$ increases, more probability weight is placed on events (0,0) and (1,1) relative to events (0,1) and (1,0). In this sense, complementary choices are associated with greater probability weight on the diagonal events of choosing both practices or neither practice. The corresponding probabilities are determined by the following three equations.

$$\Pr(M = 1, R = 0|X\beta) = \Phi(-X\beta_R - X\beta*_{MR}) \\ -\Phi_2(-X\beta_M, -X\beta_R - X\beta*_{MR}, \rho) \qquad (19)$$

$$\Pr(M = 0, R = 1|X\beta) = \Phi(-X\beta_M - X\beta*_M R) \\ -\Phi_2(-X\beta_M - X\beta*_{MR}, -X\beta_R, \rho) \qquad (20)$$

and

$$\Pr(M = 0, R = 0|X\beta) = \Phi_2(-X\beta_M - X\beta*_{MR}, -X\beta_R, \rho) \\ + \int_{-X\beta_M - X\beta*_{MR}}^{-X\beta_M} \Phi\left(\frac{-X\beta_M - X\beta_R - X\beta_{MR} - \epsilon_M(1+\rho)}{(1-\rho^2)^{\frac{1}{2}}}\right) d\epsilon_M \qquad (21)$$

where Φ is the cumulative density of the standard normal distribution and Φ_2 is the cumulative density of the standard bivariate normal distribution. The cumulative distribution that is integrated in Equation (21) is the standardized cumulative distribution of ϵ_R conditional upon a particular value of ϵ_M (the diagonal line in Figure 1). The log likelihood function is then

$$L(M, R, X\beta) = \sum_{i=1}^{n}((1 - M) \cdot (1 - R) \cdot \ln(\Pr(M = 0, R = 0|X\beta)) \\ + M \cdot (1 - R) \cdot \ln(\Pr(M = 1, R = 0|X\beta)) \\ + (1 - M) \cdot R \cdot \ln(\Pr(M = 0, R = 1|X\beta)) \\ + M \cdot R \cdot \ln(1 - \Pr(M = 0, R = 0|X\beta) \\ - \Pr(M = 1, R = 0|X\beta) - \Pr(M = 0, R = 1|X\beta)) \qquad (22)$$

where n is the number of observations. This log likelihood function can be estimated using standard maximum likelihood techniques, with the addition of a procedure to approximate the integral in Equation (21).[6] Using the standard calculus technique of Riemann integration, this integral can be approximated "from below" by the following finite sum (Browder (1996)).

$$\sum_{m=1}^{\mu} \Phi_2\left(-X\beta_M - \frac{(m-1)}{\mu}X\beta_{MR}, -X\beta_R - \frac{\mu-m+1}{\mu}X\beta_{MR}, \rho\right) \\ -\Phi_2\left(-X\beta_M - \frac{m}{\mu}X\beta_{MR}, -X\beta_R - \frac{\mu-m+1}{\mu}X\beta_{MR}, \rho\right) \qquad (23)$$

---

[6]Note that a similar model is discussed in some detail in Greene (2000, pp. 852-856), where it is called a "recursive simultaneous equations model."

The model can be consistently estimated as long as $\mu \to \infty$ as $n \to \infty$.

Summing up, if it is the case that the term $X\beta*_{MR}$ is always 0, then the model corresponds to the standard bivariate probit model that has been used previously in the literature (Jones and Pliskin (1997)). By allowing this term to be positive, extra probability weight can be placed on the "diagonal" events to use both teams and training (the event (1,1))or to use neither teams nor training (the event (0,0)). As shown above, the skewing of the probabilities and placing more weight on the diagonal events, corresponds to the two practices being complements.

The model is estimated on the data set presented in the next section.

4 Data

The data set used to analyze the firm's decision to use these high performance work systems is based on a large survey of U.S. manufacturing establishments. National Employer Survey (NES) 1994 is a stratified random sample of US private sector establishments with over 20 employees conducted by the Bureau of the Census working with the University of Pennsylvania's Center on the Educational Quality of the Workforce. The survey was administered by telephone in August and September 1994. The respondent to this survey is the plant manager. The response rate is 72 % with 3,358 establishments participating, including 1,621 manufacturing establishments.[7]

The data set has unique advantages for testing the hypotheses presented above. In particular it is a large data set that provides information on training programs, the use of human resource practices such as self-managed work teams, and information on the general characteristics of the establishments surveyed.[8] The large representative sample is necessary for understanding the adoption of human resource practices in U.S. manufacturing. Much of

---

[7]For further discussion of the data see Black and Lynch (1998). The public use data files for NES 1994 and NES 1997 may be obtained at http://www.irhe.upenn.edu/.

[8]The more recent NES 1997 data is similar to NES 1994, although it does not contain any information regarding the firm's product market. Therefore it is not appropriate for this paper.

the previous analysis is undertaken on surveys of particular industries, including steel, automobiles and apparel, leading to substantive extrapolation problems.[9] The survey design oversampled manufacturing firms and large firms (Black and Lynch (1998)) allowing for somewhat more sophisticated econometric modeling than would be possible with other data sets.

The sample used below includes 907 of the original 1,621 manufacturing firms.[10] These establishments have the following characteristics: they have over 50 employees, at least 50 % of the employees are production workers, and the respondent gave complete answers to all of the relevant survey questions. The smaller firms were dropped because these firms are less likely to use institutions such as self-managed work teams and formal training programs, simply because they are small enough and flexible enough that the increased structure is unnecessary. Therefore, for very small firms the use of particular human resource practices is a poor measure of how much decision making power is actually delegated to production line worker and how much training these workers are provided with. Firms with a smaller proportion of production workers were dropped because the question on the use of self-managed work teams asks about "non-managerial and non-supervisory" employees, while the question on training asked specifically about production workers.

The analysis uses two dependent variables: whether self-managed work teams are used and whether formal training programs are used. Both are dichotomous variables. TEAMS is 1 if the respondent answered that more than 10 % of "non-managerial and non-supervisory employees are currently involved in self-managed teams" and 0 if less than 10 % of these employees are currently involved in self-managed teams. By assuming that firms with less than 10 % of employees in self-managed work teams are *not* using them, the measure states that the firms using the practice are the ones that have made a substantial commitment. Such firms have considerably altered their decision making structure to delegate more decision making power to the

---

[9]Noteworthy exceptions include Osterman (1994, 1995) and Black and Lynch (1998).

[10]The survey actually sampled individual establishments within firms. However, for the most part the paper uses the terms "establishment" and "firm" interchangeably.

production line workers.[11]

TRAINING is 1 if the respondent answered that some number of production workers have received formal instruction in the last year. TRAINING is 0 if no production workers have received formal instruction in the last year. Formal instruction includes "structured or formal training either on-the-job (by supervisors or outside contractors) or at a school or technical institute". This definition is meant to capture those training programs that do more than simply show the worker how to perform the required tasks, but also increase the decision making ability of the production line worker. It would be preferable to have information on the proportion of production workers involved in these training programs in order to have a better idea of the penetration. Unfortunately that information is not available in this data set.[12]

The analysis uses two measures of the firm's product market. CUSTOM is 1 if the respondent answered that tailoring its products to specific customer needs is the most important way to compete in the firm's product market. CUSTOM is 0 if the respondent answered that some *other* method is the most important way to compete in the product market. QUALITY is 1 if the respondent stated that producing quality products is the best way for the establishment to compete in its product market. QUALITY is 0 is some *other* method is the most important way to compete.[13]

The proxy for the volatility of the firm's product market (α) is CUSTOM. Rewriting Hypothesis 1 in terms of this measure, the hypothesis is supported if the following two equations hold.

$$\beta_{CUSTOMM} > 0 \qquad (24)$$

---

[11]It would be preferable to use a higher cutoff (say 50 %), but the data set is not large enough to allow that possibility. See Osterman (1994, 1995) for further discussions of the penetration of human resource practices.

[12]While the data provides information on the number of production workers who have received training, it does not provide information on the number of production workers there are in the firm.

[13]The other major answer to this was question is price.

and
$$\beta_{CUSTOMM} + \beta*_{CUSTOMMR} > 0 \qquad (25)$$

If the firm states that tailoring its product to specific customer needs is the most important way to compete then such a firm is likely to have many different products on the production line and a lot of day to day changes on the best method to use in completing the order. One concern with this proxy and with the related measure QUALITY is that the respondent was asked to choose the "best" answer, and so there may be firms that compete both on customized products and quality, but choose quality because that is the "most important" way the firm competes. It would be preferable to have much more detailed information about how much change is occurring on the production line, rather than making inferences from general characteristics of the firm's product market.

A number papers in the literature suggest that firms that produce high QUALITY products will more likely to use employee involvement programs such as TEAMS (Arthur (1994); Eaton and Voos (1992); Osterman (1994)). It also seems reasonable that firms that produce high QUALITY products will be more likely to use TRAINING programs in order to increase the skill of the workforce. This explanation for the use of training differs from the explanation presented in the theory section. It would be preferable to have more information on the nature of the training programs used by these firms. Do these programs improve decision making? Do they simply improve the worker's skill? Do they do both? Training programs that do different things will be used for different reasons, unfortunately the data does not allow the researcher distinguish between the different types of training programs.

The analysis uses four other measures of firm characteristics. UNION is 1 if there is at least one union in the establishment. UNION is 0 if there is no union in the establishment. Previous work suggests that the existence of unions decreases the likelihood that the firm will use TEAMS (Osterman (1994)) and increases the likelihood of using TRAINING programs (Adams (2001); Black and Lynch (1998); Osterman (1995)). It is argued in the literature that unions tend to appose the use of practices (like self-managed

Variable	Percentage
Firms that use self-managed work teams (TEAMS)	22
Firms that use formal training programs (TRAINING)	77
Firms that tailor products to customer needs (CUSTOM)	27
Firms that produce high quality products (QUALITY)	35
Firms with at least one union (UNION)	26
Firms with 50 to 99 employees (50TO99)	48
Firms with 100 to 249 Employees (100TO249)	32
Firms with multiple establishments (MULTI)	59

Table 1: Frequencies

work teams) that reduce their bargaining power, particularly practices that increase the flexibility of the firm to move workers from job to job. Unions may support training programs that improve the workers skill and human capital, but may not support training programs that increase worker flexibility. 50TO99 is 1 if there are less than 100 employees in the establishment (note that all establishments have at least 50 employees). 50TO99 is 0 if the establishment has 100 or greater employees. 100TO249 is 1 if the establishment has between 100 and 249 employees. 100TO249 is 0 if there are less than 100 employees or more than 249. MULTI is 1 if this establishment is part of a firm with multiple establishments. MULTI is 0 if this establishment is the only establishment in the firm. All three variables measure the size of the firm. Results from previous work suggests larger firms are more likely to use both TEAMS and TRAINING (Adams (2001); Black and Lynch (1998); Osterman (1994, 1995)). As argued above, using these formal human resource practices in small firms is often unnecessary.

Table 1 shows the frequencies for each of the variables in the data set. TEAMS are used by 22 % of firms and TRAINING is used by 77 % of firms. The measures of characteristics of the product market are CUSTOM and QUALITY, with 27 % categorized as the first and 35 % categorized as the second. The rest of the table shows that 26 % of establishments are unionized, almost half have less than 100 employees and 59 % belong to firms with more than one establishment.

5 Results

Table 2 presents the results of the model.[14] To test Hypothesis 1 the appropriate equation is Equation (24),

$$\beta_{CUSTOMM} = .30 > 0 \tag{26}$$

which is statistically significantly different from 0, and Equation (25) is,

$$\beta_{CUSTOMM} + \beta*_{CUSTOMMR} = .30 - .02 = .28 > 0 \tag{27}$$

which is also statistically significant. These results give support for Hypothesis 1, and suggest that conditional on the use of TRAINING, firms value the use of TEAMS more highly when there is volatility on the firm's production floor.

To test Hypothesis 2 the appropriate equation is,

$$\beta*_{CUSTOMMR} + \beta*_{CONSTANT} = -.02 + .85 = .83 > 0 \tag{28}$$

The alternative hypothesis is that this equation is always 0, is equivalent to a standard bivariate probit model. A log-likelihood ratio test between the model presented above and the standard bivariate probit model, shows that the test statistic is 10.92, which is statistically significant. This result supports Hypothesis 2 and suggests that firms view TEAMS and TRAINING as complements.

Overall these results support the hypotheses presented above. The results show that whether the firm produces customized products has a positive effect on the probability that the firm uses TEAMS. The probability (unconditional on the use of TRAINING programs) that the firm uses TEAMS is

---

[14]These particular results are from a model in which $\mu = 100$ (see Equation (23)), although the results vary little from the results in which $\mu = 2$.

Variable			$\frac{\partial Prob}{\partial x}$
Teams ($X\beta_M$)			
Custom	.30	(.11)	.10
Quality	.18	(.10)	.05
Union	-.16	(.10)	-.04
50to99	-.22	(.11)	-.06
100to249	-.28	(.12)	-.08
Multi	.14	(.09)	.04
Constant	.04	(.13)	-
Training ($X\beta_R$)			
Custom	.43	(.12)	.13
Quality	.28	(.09)	.10
Union	-.23	(.09)	-.09
50to99	-.25	(.10)	-.08
100to249	-.24	(.11)	-.06
Multi	.19	(.08)	.07
Constant	.77	(.13)	-
Both ($X\beta*_{MR}$)			
Custom	-.02	(.07)	
Constant	.85	(.03)	
ρ	.9990		
Log likelihood	-911.68		

Table 2: Bivariate Probit with Complementarity (standard errors)

10 percentage points higher for firms that believe tailoring the product to customer needs is the best way to compete in the their product market. This is the largest effect on the probability of using self-managed work teams of any of the observable characteristics. The results also show that the use of TRAINING has a large positive effect on the firm's propensity to choose TEAMS. If the mean firm does *not* use TRAINING, then it chooses TEAMS with 7 % probability. However, if the mean firm does use TRAINING, then it chooses TEAMS with 25 % probability.[15]

These results also give some support for the claim that firms that produce high quality products will be more likely to use self-managed work teams. However, the mean firm is only 5 % more likely to use self-managed work teams if it produces a quality product, and the coefficient is not statistically significantly different from 0. As suspected above, firms that produce QUALITY products are more likely to use TRAINING. The reason is that some of these training programs improve the skill of the workers. Similar to previous results in the literature, firms with unions are less likely to use self-managed work teams and larger firms are more likely to use both self-managed work teams and formal training programs (Adams (2001); Black and Lynch (1998); Osterman (1994, 1995)). However, unlike in earlier papers, firms with unions are *less* likely to use formal training programs (Adams (2001); Black and Lynch (1998); Osterman (1995)). Black and Lynch (1998) use the same data but find that firms with unions are more likely to use formal training programs although the estimated coefficient is not statistically significantly different from 0. A possible explanation for the discrepancy is that the model estimated by Black and Lynch (1998) includes the use of self-managed work teams an explanatory variable, even though it may be simultaneously chosen and complementary to the use of formal training programs.

One issue with these estimation results is the unusually large estimate for ρ. Note that ρ is bounded above by 1. As discussed above, when ρ increases it skews the distribution on to the diagonal (places greater probability weight

---

[15]These probabilities are *not* presented in Table 2. They are calculated by inserting the estimated parameters back into the model and calculating the effect of forcing $R = 0$ and $R = 1$ respectively.

on events using both practices and using neither practice). This result then suggests that there are other unmeasured factors that affect the degree to which these practices are complements.[16]

6 Conclusion

The literature suggests that the use of high performance work systems leads to productivity improvements in at least some manufacturing industries (Appelbaum et al. (2000); Ichniowski et al. (1997)). One concern with these types of results is the observation that firms are not randomly adopting these practices leading to biased results. This paper attempts to better understand why firms adopt particular high performance work practices and whether firms are more likely to adopt groups of practices (or systems of practices). The paper analyzes the adoption of two important human resource practices, self-managed work teams and formal training programs. The paper has two important results. The first result shows that particular types of firms value particular practices more highly, for example firms that produce customized products place greater value on the use of teams. The second result shows that self-managed work teams and formal training programs are complements, and therefore are more likely to be chosen in combination as part of "work systems."

The paper analyzes a theoretical model to better understand the mechanism via which a manufacturing firm would value the use of self-managed work teams and the use of formal training programs, both independently and in combination with each other. The use of self-managed work teams is modelled as the decision to take decision making power away from a production manager or production engineer (an "off-line" decision maker) and give that decision making power to a production line worker (an "on-line"

---

[16]Adams (2001) shows that in the analysis of Australian data, when other measures are added to the $X\beta*_{MR}$ equation, the estimate for ρ decreases. Adams (2001) also shows that the value of ρ decreases when an extra error term (ϵ_{iMR}) is allowed to be non-zero and correlated with the other error terms. Note further that if $\rho = 1$, then the model corresponds to a particular example of the ordered probit model.

decision maker). The model illustrates the trade-off between the fast decisions of the on-line decision maker and slow but more educated decisions of the off-line decision maker. There are two main theoretical results. The first result states that conditional on whether the firm uses training, firms value the use of teams more when there is a lot of volatility on the production floor, relative to when there is little volatility. The second result states that teams and training programs are complements. Hypotheses based on these two theoretical results are tested on a data set based on a large survey of U.S. manufacturing establishments.

An empirical model is presented that is more general than models used in previous work (for example Jones and Pliskin (1997)). This model allows the firm to choose to adopt both teams and training programs simultaneously and it allows the choices to interact and for this interaction to vary across firms. The results of the empirical analysis give support for the two hypotheses. In regards to the first hypothesis, the results show that conditional on the use of training programs, firms that produce custom products value the use of teams more highly than firms that don't. It is argued in the paper that firms that produce custom products will face greater volatility on the production floor. In regards to the second hypothesis, the results show that an empirical model that allows for a positive interaction term between the two choices is more likely given the data than a model which allows for no interaction. It is shown in the paper, that this test is equivalent to testing for whether the two practices are complements.

These results suggest caution in interpreting the estimated productivity effects of using "high performance work systems." Firm's choose practices systematically and this selection of practices must be accounted for in the empirical analysis.

7 Appendix

Proof of Proposition 1. (1). The proof has two parts. Part (i) shows that there exists an α_l such that for $\alpha < \alpha_l$, $V_{10} - V_{00} < 0$. Part (ii) shows that there exists an α_h such that for $\alpha_h < \alpha$, $V_{10} - V_{00} > 0$.

i) Let $\gamma_R = 1$. The off-line decision maker's belief at time t is one of two values,
$$\omega_t = \begin{cases} r^2(0) & \text{if } s_{t-2} = 0 \\ r^2(1) & \text{if } s_{t-2} = 1 \end{cases} \tag{29}$$
where $r(s_t) = (1-\alpha)s_t + \alpha(1-s_t)$. As $\alpha \to 0$ the off-line decision maker knows the state and always makes the correct choice. By Claim 5 Rustichini and Wolinsky (1995), $\lim_{\alpha \to 0}$ the stationary probability that $\tau_t = 0$ given $s_t = 1$ is strictly positive (ie, that the on-line chooses the incorrect task). So as $\alpha \to 0$, $V_{10} < V_{00}$, and thus there exists such an α_l. The Proof of Proposition 2, shows V_{10} is non-increasing in γ_R, and by assumption V_{00} is constant in γ_R.

ii) There are two cases. Case 1) Let $k < 0.5$. Let $\gamma_R = 1$. Let α_h be such that $r^2(0) = k$, that is
$$\alpha_h = \frac{2 - (4-8k)^{\frac{1}{2}}}{4} \tag{30}$$
By Claim 2 (Rustichini and Wolinsky (1995)), if
$$\frac{1}{k} \geq \frac{2(1 - \delta_d(1-2\alpha))\log \delta_d}{2\alpha \log \delta_d - (1-\delta_d)(1-2\alpha)\log(1-2\alpha)} \tag{31}$$
Then $\tau_t = 1$ for all t. Let α_3 be such that Equation (31) holds with equality. We know $\alpha_h < \alpha_3$ as at α_h, Equation (31) does not hold. At α_h, $V_{00} = \frac{1}{2}$ and at α_3, $V_{10} = \frac{1}{2}$. We know that for $\alpha < \alpha_3$, $\tau_t \neq 1$ for all t and therefore by revealed preference $\sum_{j=t}^{\infty} \delta_d^{j-t} \Pr(\pi_j | \omega_t) > \frac{1}{2}$ for all δ_d and so $V_{10} > \frac{1}{2} = V_{00}$. Let $\gamma_R < 1$. The result holds for large enough γ_R as by definition V_W is continuous in γ_R. The rest follows in a similar fashion to Case (1). Case 2) Let $k \geq 0.5$. Let $\gamma_R = 1$. Let α_h be such that $r^2(1) = k$, so
$$\alpha_h = \frac{2 - (4-8(1-k))^{\frac{1}{2}}}{4} \tag{32}$$
By Claim 2 Rustichini and Wolinsky (1995) if
$$\frac{1}{k} \leq 2 - \delta_d(1-2\alpha) \tag{33}$$

then $\tau_t = 0$ for all t. Let α_3 be such that Equation (33) holds with equality. At α_h, Equation (33) does not hold if

$$\delta_d > \frac{(2k-1)^{\frac{1}{2}}}{k} \tag{34}$$

By a similar argument to Case (1), if Equation (34) holds $\alpha_h < \alpha_3$ and at α_h, $V_{10} > V_{00}$. Let $\gamma_R < 1$. For large enough γ_R, the result holds as V_{10} is continuous in γ_R.

(2). The proof is identical to the proof of (1), replacing V_{10} with V_{11} and V_{00} with V_{01}. QED.

Proof of Proposition 2. Let $\gamma_1 = \gamma_0$. Then $V_{00} = V_{01}$ and $V_{10} = V_{11}$ and so $V_{00} + V_{11} = V_{01} + V_{10}$. The proof follows by showing that

$$\frac{\partial((V_{00} + V_{11}) - (V_{01} + V_{10})}{\partial \gamma_1} > 0 \tag{35}$$

Noting that $\gamma_1 > \gamma_0$. By assumption, only V_{11} is a function of γ_1, therefore it is sufficient to show that $\frac{\partial V_{11}}{\partial \gamma_1} > 0$. Consider some period t, Adams (2001) (Lemma 2) shows that assuming δ_f is close to 1 is equivalent to assuming that firm values the decision maker by looking at the average distribution over a large number of periods.

$$V_{11} = \lim_{T \to \infty} \frac{1}{T} \Sigma_{j=t}^{t+T} (\Pr(\tau_j = 0|\omega_t)k + \Pr(\tau_j = 1 \text{ and } s_j = 1|\omega_t)) \tag{36}$$

The derivative of V_{11} with respect to γ_1 has two parts. First, $\frac{\partial \Pr(\tau_j=1 \text{ and } s_j=1|\omega_t)}{\partial \gamma}$ can be re-written as $E(\Pr(\omega_j > W | s_j = 1, \omega_{j-1})|\omega_t)$, where W is the on-line decision maker's "cut-off" belief (Adams (2001), Lemma 1). By assumption, there exists some j such that $\tau_{j-1} = 1$. Let ω^1 be the belief if $\tau_{j-1} = 1$ and $\sigma_{11j} = 0$ and let ω^2 be the belief if $\tau_{j-1} = 1$ and $\sigma_{11j} = 1$. Given ω_{j-1}, there are three cases:
1) $\omega^1 \leq \omega^2 \leq W$,
2) $W \leq \omega^1 \leq \omega^2$, and
3) $\omega^1 < W < \omega^2$,

In cases (1) and (2), nothing changes with an increase in γ_1, but it is also true that the on-line decision maker learns nothing from choosing $\tau_{j-1} = 1$. By assumption, case (3) must hold at least some of the time. If $\tau_{j-1} = 1$, consider case (3) and let $s_j = 1$, then

$$\Pr(\omega_j > W) = (1 - \alpha)\gamma_1 + \alpha(1 - \gamma_1) \tag{37}$$

this is because $\Pr(s_{j-1} = 1) = 1 - \alpha$, and if $s_{j-1} = 1$ then $\pi_{t-1} = 1$ and $\Pr(\sigma_j = 1) = \gamma_1$. We thus have that

$$\frac{\partial \Pr(\omega_j > W)}{\partial \gamma_1} = 1 - 2\alpha > 0 \tag{38}$$

Note that $\alpha \in (0, .5)$.

Similarly, we can look at $\frac{\partial \Pr(\tau_j = 0 | \omega_t)}{\partial \gamma_1}$. If $\tau_{j-1} = 1$, Case (3) holds and $s_j = 0$, then

$$\Pr(\omega_j < W) = (1 - \alpha)\gamma_1 + \alpha(1 - \gamma_1) \tag{39}$$

and

$$\frac{\partial \Pr(\omega_j < W)}{\partial \gamma_1} = 1 - 2\alpha > 0 \tag{40}$$

QED.

References

Adams, Christopher, "Theory and Practice of Shopfloor Decision Making in Manufacturing." PhD dissertation, University of Wisconsin–Madison 2001.

Appelbaum, Eileen, Thomas Bailey, Peter Berg, and Arne Kalleberg, *Manufacturing Advantage: Why High Performance Work Systems Pay Off*, Cornell University Press, 2000.

Arthur, Jeffrey, "Effects of Human Resource Systems on Manufacturing Performance and Turnover," *Academy of Management Journal*, 1994, *37* (3), 670–687.

Athey, Susan and Scott Stern, "An Empirical Framework for Testing Theories About Complexity in Organizational Design," April 1998. April draft.

Black, Sandra and Lisa Lynch, "Beyond the Incidence of Employer-Provided Training," *Industrial and Labor Relations Review*, October 1998, *52* (1), 64–82.

Borland, Jeff and Jurgen Eichberger, "Organizational Form Outside the Principal-Agent Paradigm," *Bulletin of Economic Research*, 1998, *50* (3).

Browder, Andrew, *Mathematical Analysis: An Introduction*, Springer, 1996.

Che, Yeon-Koo and Seung-Weon Yoo, "Optimal Incentives for Teams," *American Economic Review*, Forthcoming.

Derman, Cyrus, *Finite State Markovian Decision Processes*, Academic Press, 1970.

Drago, Robert, "Measures of Employee Participation: A Background Paper for the 1995 Australian Workplace Industrial Relations Survey," 1995. Draft.

Eaton, Adrienne and Paula Voos, "Union and Contemporary Innovations in Work Organizations, Compensation, and Employee Participation," in Lawrence Mishel and Paula Voos, eds., *Unions and the Economic Competitiveness*, M. E. Sharp, 1992, pp. 175–215.

_ , _ , **and Dong-one Kim**, "Voluntary and Involuntary Aspects of Employee Participation in Decision Making," in David Levine, Daniel Mitchell, and Mahmood Zaidi, eds., *The Human Resource Management Handbook (Part 1)*, JAI Press, 1997, pp. 63–85.

Ichniowski, Casey, Kathryn Shaw, and Giovanna Prennushi, "The Effects of Human Resource Management Practices on Productivity: A

Study of Steel Finishing Lines," *American Economic Review*, 1997, *87*, 291–313.

Jones, Derek and Jeffrey Pliskin, "Determinants of the Incidence of Group Incentives: Evidence from Canada," *Canadian Journal of Economics*, November 1997, *30* (4b), 1027–1045.

Kandel, Eugene and Edward Lazear, "Peer Pressure and Partnerships," *Journal of Political Economy*, 1992, *100*, 801–817.

Levine, David, *Reinventing the Workplace: How Business and Employees Can Both Win*, The Brookings Institution, 1995.

Milgrom, Paul and John Roberts, "The Economics of Modern Manufacturing: Technology, Strategy, and Organization," *The American Economic Review*, June 1990, pp. 511–528.

Osterman, Paul, "How Common is Workplace Transformation and Who Adopts It?," *Industrial and Labor Relations Review*, 1994, *47*, 173–187.

_ , "Skill, Training, and Work Organizations in American Establishments," *Industrial Relations*, April 1995, *34* (2).

Puterman, Martin, *Markov Decision Processes: Discrete Stochastic Dynamic Programming*, John Wiley and Sons, 1994.

Rustichini, Aldo and Asher Wolinsky, "Learning About Variable Demand in the Long Run," *Journal of Economic Dynamics and Control*, 1995, *19*, 1283–1292.

Stokey, Nancy L. and Robert E. Lucas, *Recursive methods in economic dynamics*, Cambridge, Mass. and London: Harvard University Press, 1989. with Edward C. Prescott.

Whitfield, Keith, "High-Performance Workplaces, Training and the Distribution of Skills," *Industrial Relations*, 2000, *39* (1).

www.ingramcontent.com/pod-product-compliance
Lightning Source LLC
Chambersburg PA
CBHW081820170526
45167CB00008B/3481